The Little Book

of

Heroin

The Little Book of Heroin

Franics Moraes, Ph.D.

Ronin Publishing
Berkeley, Ca
www.roninpub.com

The Little Book of Heroin

Paper isbn: 9780914171980
Ebook isbn: 9781579511984

Published by
RONIN Publishing, Inc.
PO Box 3436
Oakland CA 94609
www.roninpub.com

Editor:Phillip Smith
Illustrations: Andrea English
Cover Design: Judy July, Generic Typography
Printer: Lightning Source

Printed in the United States
Distributed by PGW/Ingram

Library of Congress Number: 99-068961

Acknowledgements

Many people helped in making this book available to a general audience. First, I thank my wife Debra for her almost constant tutelage in human biology. Andrea English provided the original artwork for this book. Jim Hogshire was, as always, enlightening. My parents provided financial support. Finally, thanks to Ronin Publishing, for believing in the First Amendment and putting this important, albeit controversial, information into print.

Notice to Readers:

Information presented in this book is made available under the First Amendment of the Constitution. It is a general overview of heroin—it's history and use—and should not be considered medical or legal advice. Possession of poppies, heroin and any of its precursors is a criminal offense. Besides being illegal, use of heroin is dangerous. The publisher and author do not advocate using drugs or breaking the law in any way. The intention in making this material available is to help friends and family of heroin users to better understand it and to aid in reducing harm to users.

Table of Contents

Foreword

For the general population, heroin is not a chemical—it is a myth. "Heroin," along with "crack" and "gang," is a word that is defined almost entirely by emotion. And yet, heroin is quite simply a chemical—a chemical that people voluntarily ingest, or in the vast majority of cases, choose not to ingest. It is fascinating how most people fear heroin when it cannot force itself onto a person. A murderer may take your life away, but heroin can affect you only if you choose to use it.

Probably, the reasons people fear heroin are the same reasons they fear Satan. Heroin is thought of as an active agent that entices unsuspecting victims into its net with initial pleasures of the flesh only to have these pleasures replaced by a life of slavery and misery once the victim is ensnared. One would think that this would cause people to wish to know more about heroin, but sadly, the main knowledge people possess about this drug is incorrect or greatly exaggerated—and almost never questioned.

The intention in writing this book is to provide information that enables the general reader to see heroin in a more objective light. In doing this, information is provided from the sciences as it applies to heroin. The physical sciences teach us what makes heroin heroin, how it is distinguished from the other opiates, and how heroin affects the human body. The social sciences teach us how heroin affects the mind—what it does for the user, how the user interacts with society, and how society views the users.

One of the most startling facts you will come across in this book is that many heroin addicts, or "junkies" are they are called, take time and care to purify the adulterated heroin they buy on the black market and to search out clean syringes. For most people, this is completely counter to everything they "know" about junkies.

The purpose of this book is to educate readers in such matters, so that you will better understand that junkies are often are thought of as a simple stereotype instead of complicated human beings who reason and feel.

This book represents an important step in the *harm reduction* movement as applied to heroin. Heroin users, their friends and family, and professionals in many fields will find much in this book that will be of help in mitigating the harm done to users of this drug. Straight-forward and objective drug education, like that found in this book, really does have the power to save lives.

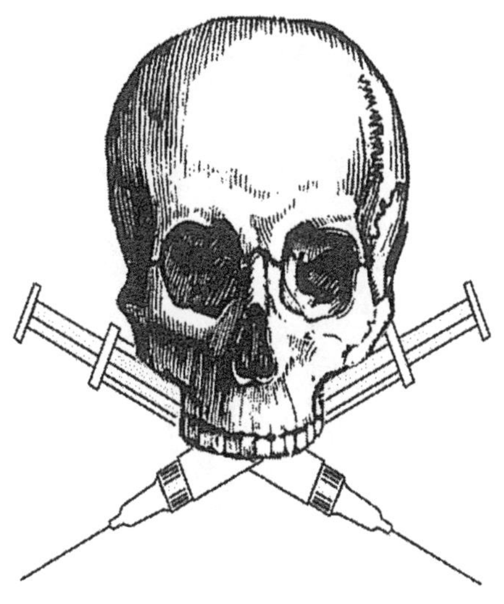

Chapter 1

What Is Heroin?

Heroin is the "brand name" of the chemical diacetylmorphine HCl, a very close relative of morphine. Surprising as it may sound, heroin has no effect on the human body. It simply acts as a transport vehicle for morphine and, to a lesser extent, codeine.

Heroin is Morphine

The process of "getting high" has two steps. In the first step, the drug must be transported to the circulatory system. This transport may be direct, as when a user injects the drug into a vein, or it may be indirect, as when the drug is eaten. Different drugs have various efficiencies when administered via different routes. Alcohol, for example, is relatively easily transported into the bloodstream via the oral (eaten) route. Heroin, on the other hand, is particularly inefficient when ingested in this manner—even when compared with morphine.

Blood-Brain Barrier

The second step in the transport of a drug is its delivery from the bloodstream to the brain. In order for this to be accomplished, the drug must pass through what is known as the "blood-brain barrier". Once the drug has crossed this barrier, the user gets whatever effects the drug produces. It is in this step that heroin is more effective than morphine. Heroin crosses the blood-brain barrier a few times more quickly than does morphine.

Heroin is Not the High

After heroin has reached the brain, it does not affect the brain directly. It just "hangs out," waiting for some chemical to react with it and strip away its diacetyl group.

When this happens, the heroin molecule becomes a morphine molecule, which has profound effects on the human body. But this point is important: heroin is a transport chemical—it does not get the user high.

It is kind of like the car that brings the keg of beer to the party. No one is going to get high sucking on the fenders of the car. Heroin is the car; morphine is the beer: morphine is what gets you high. Because of this property of heroin, when talking about its chemical aspects we are actually discussing morphine.

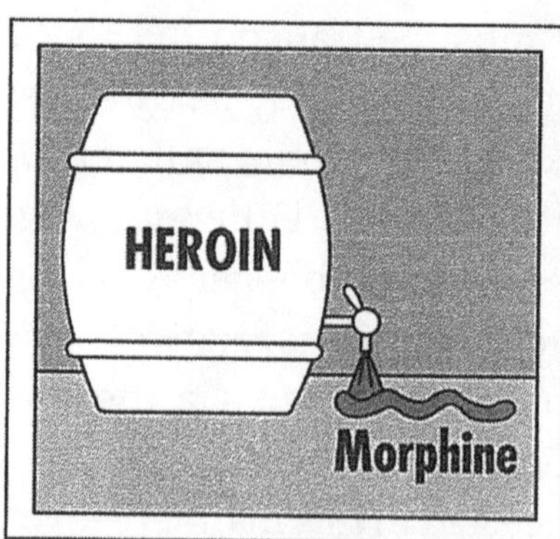

Heroin transports morphine to the brain, just as a keg transports beer to a bar or party .

Why Heroin?

Many people wonder why addicts use heroin instead of morphine if they are the same thing. There are two reasons.

The first is that transport and distribution of illegal substances requires the smallest and most potent form of the substance—which in this case would be heroin. During Prohibition, the primary form of alcohol was whisky; today it is beer. Distributors need to transport 20 times as much 3% alcohol beer as they do 120 proof whisky. When the opioids were legal, addicts usually *drank* opium in various concoctions such as tinctures. Now that they are illegal, addicts usually *inject* heroin.

The second reason that the illegal opioid trade doesn't distribute morphine as that it is very easy to convert morphine into heroin. There are even more potent opioids than heroin. Dilaudid"®, for example, is almost three times as potent as heroin. But it is a lot harder to create Dilaudid"® than heroin. So heroin is a compromise between high potency and low effort on the part of the distributors.

Effects of Morphine

Describing the psychological effects of morphine is very difficult, because they are quite subtle.

Euphoria

Morphine does not make the user happy, as LSD often does, with the user giggling and childlike. Instead, the user is filled with a sense of safety and contentment, largely because of the drug's action of depressing the *locus coeruleus* of the brain, which controls alarm signals, called the "fight or flight" response.

The fact that the euphoria is subtle should not be taken to mean that it is not profound—there is a reason that people become addicted to it. The feeling has often been likened to heaven. In fact, the band, Talking Heads recorded a song called *Heaven* that captures this feeling perfectly when it talks about being perfectly contented just sitting around listening to the same song over and over.

Opiate Receptor Sites

This happiness and contentment is not only the product of a depressed locus coeruleus. In fact, the feelings of euphoria come from the stimulation of opiate receptor sites. These are areas in the brain, spinal cord, intestines, and possibly elsewhere. Chemicals that the body produces called "opioid peptides" or "endorphins" attach to the body's opiate receptor sites and make the body feel good. Morphine is a very similar chemical to the endorphins, so it also acts on the brain in the same way.

Heroin Rush

Athletes sometimes experience what is called a "rush" when their bodies suddenly release a large number of endorphins. This is called the "runner's high,"which is quite similar to another pleasurable effect of heroin use: *the rush.*

This is a short period (less than five minutes) where the opiate receptor sites are inundated with morphine resulting in an intense joy. This feeling has been likened to a very long orgasm. But the experience is very personal—experienced differently by different people and differently by a single person at different times.

This "heroin rush" requires a large amount of morphine to be delivered to the brain in a small amount of time. As a result, it is mainly users who administer the drug through intravenous injection who experience it. Very skilled smokers can also experience the rush, but those who inhale—snort—or swallow do not.

Cognition

Morphine does not have a great effect on the cognitive abilities, because it acts on the lower brain and brain stem—the parts of the brain that are responsible for automatic functions like breathing—and not the higher brain. However, morphine does cause the user to think much more slowly. A common example of this is when a user is riding in a car and complains that the driver is tailgating. Generally, this would not be the case for a sober driver, but a driver under the influence of morphine's slower thinking requires a great deal more time to react to environmental changes such as slowing cars.

Nausea

For most new users—and many long-time ones—the first and most obvious effect of morphine is nausea with vomiting. Some users experience no nausea whatsoever. But for the repeat user who does, nausea is a side-effect—one that is palatable because of the pleasurable effects of morphine. In fact, some users come to enjoy vomiting because of its association with the euphoria that follows it.

Depressed Respiration

The most profound physical effect of morphine is its depression of the respiratory system. This makes heroin an excellent cough suppressant, though it is not usually ingested for this reason today.

Overdosing

When a user overdoses, it is because of this effect —most deaths involving heroin are not overdoses. With a true overdose, the victim's respiration is greatly lowered and eventually stops altogether. It generally takes at least an hour for the user to die from an overdose, so if others are around, medical attention can be given to save the victim's life.

Constipation

The last of the major physical effects of morphine is its ability to constipate. All of the opioids are excellent constipating agents. In fact, the first written reference to opium concerns its usefulness as a cure for diarrhea.

Even today, Imodium®, a non-psychoactive opioid, is about the best treatment for diarrhea. The flip side of this effect is that when the body becomes physically addicted to morphine and then is denied it, extreme diarrhea often ensues, because the body is used to over-compensating for the presence of morphine.

Other Physical Effects

Morphine causes a number of other minor physical changes. These include difficulty urinating and extreme constriction of the pupils.

Later in this book we will look at the effects that heroin addiction and the addict lifestyle may have on the user's body, but in terms of direct effects of the drug, this is about it. The opioids—including morphine and, of course, heroin—are fairly gentle on the human body and brain. The laws and social mythology of heroin create its greatest dangers.

Chapter 2

History of Heroin

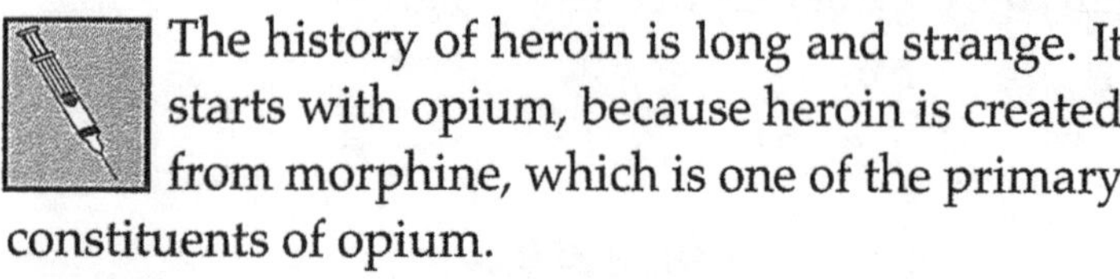

The history of heroin is long and strange. It starts with opium, because heroin is created from morphine, which is one of the primary constituents of opium.

Opium

Opium is a poorly defined substance. Whereas morphine is a single chemical entity, opium is a chemical soup which is made up of roughly forty different alkaloids. The most important of these are morphine, codeine, and thebaine.

Codeine is similar in action to morphine though it is less euphoric. Thebaine has no narcotic properties; its primary effect is nausea, but it is used widely in the manufacture of semi-synthetic opioids.

Technically speaking, opium can only be extracted from the oriental poppy, call *Papaver somniferum*. However, pseudo opium, containing varying amounts of morphine, may be created from many kinds of poppies. In all cases, this is done by air drying the juice from the seed pods of the flowers.

Uses of Opium

Papaver somniferum , also called "The Oriental Poppy", produces opium juice.

Opium has been used for at least a few thousand years—primarily as a cure for diarrhea, but also for its pain-relieving and euphoria-producing qualities.

Over its lifetime opium has been a controversial substance. In fact, a war was fought over opium by England and China—though this war had far more to do with economics than it did with the pharmacology of opium.

Overall, opium and its powerful alkaloids had a good reputation over the ages. Opioids remain the most important analgesics—non-sleep-producing pain relievers—after aspirin. At the end of the 20th century, with the most recent—and serious—drug war, all opioids have become suspect, although their medical benefits are still unquestioned.

Heroin is the great exception. Since 1926 it has been completely illegal in the United States—which means that the government believes that it has no usefulness at all. Even today, heroin is legally available in only a handful of countries. These great legal restrictions on heroin are the result of public associations with death and moral degeneracy.

The chemical heroin differs in no important sense from morphine, but the history and current status of heroin have little to do with its pharmacology and almost everything to do with perceptions.

The Early Days

In 1874, British chemist C.R.A. Wright invented the chemical diacetylmorphine HCl by boiling morphine with acetic anhydride, a weak acid chemically similar to vinegar.

Carl Duisberg of the Bayer Chemical Company pulled heroin out of obscurity and pushed it into worldwide prominence.

Little notice was taken of this new compound for more than twenty years. In the middle 1890s, Carl Duisberg of the German chemical company Bayer happened upon Wright's description of this new drug and set to work on it.

Cough Suppressant

At that time, there was a great need for effective cough suppressants. In the middle of the nineteenth century, tuberculosis was the number one killer in Europe and the United States—responsible for one-fifth of all deaths. The first property noted of heroin was its effectiveness at reducing respiration and thus stopping coughs. As a result of this, heroin was marketed as a cough suppressant to the large and waiting customer base. It was popular with doctors and patients alike. In 1900 heroin, along with aspirin, was the focus of the Bayer enterprise.

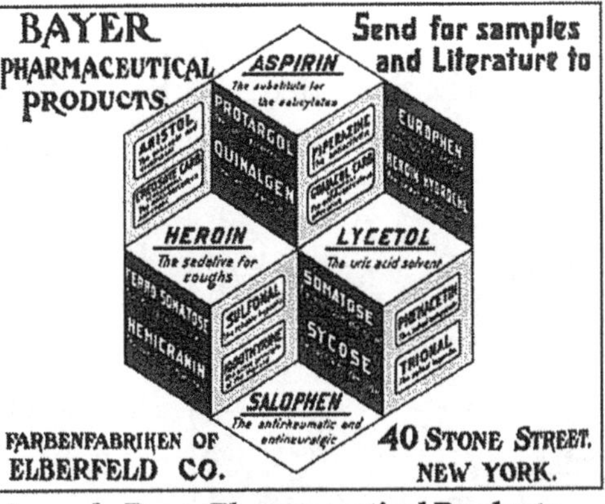

An early Bayer Pharmaceutical Products advertisement featuring heroin as a cough suppressant.

Vilification

It was not long, however, before things began to change. In the nineteenth century, relatively little notice was taken of opium and its derivatives in western countries. Public concern was focused on the effects of alcohol. This makes a certain amount of sense, even though the negative effects of alcohol on society were less at that time than they are today. Alcohol makes people more outgoing with the effect that many people are more prone to exhibit violence against others—particularly their spouses.

Temperence Movement

The temperance movements of the time were more concerned with social degeneration and the purity of the body than they were with any real concern about drinkers. But the mythic and the practical can merge synergistically to greatly influence opinion, as indicted by the passage of the Volstead Act in 1919, which marked the beginning of Prohibition.

That those in the temperance movement should also vilify other drugs with the same mythic notions should come as no surprise. In fact, the de facto leader of the temperance movement, Richmond Pearson Hobson, hardly missed a beat after the passage of the Volstead Act in turning his attack squarely against the opioids. Within ten years, heroin was eradicated from America, at least as far as the lawmakers were concerned. In fact, there are far more addicts today than there were at the time heroin was legally vilified.

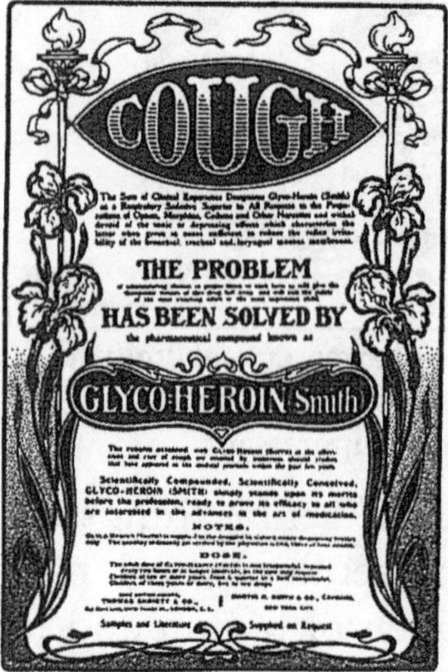

The first medicinal use of heroin was to reduce respiration and thus suppress coughing.

Political Agenda

Hobson and his temperance followers were not solely responsibly for turning public opinion against heroin and the other opioids. Others had been doing this for many years for very different reasons. Perhaps the most important was Samuel Gompers, president of the American Federation of Labor (AFL, as in AFL-CIO).

In the late 19th century, American labor was afraid of the flux of Chinese laborers who were coming into the country. These laborers were both more productive and willing to work longer hours. American labor's response: they've got to go.

During the last half of the 19th century, the vilification of the Chinese and of opium went hand in hand. When the opioids became controlled under the Harrison Narcotics Act of 1914, it was much more a result of racism directed toward Chinese immigrants than a response to concern about the effects of these drugs.

Of course, the Chinese were not the only people so treated. Reading the congressional debate regarding the Harrison Act is a real eye-opener. The debates included pointed racist attacks on the behavior of southern blacks as a reason for the control of cocaine.

Later, Harry Anslinger, head of the Federal Bureau of Narcotics, associated marijuana—a name designed for this purpose—with Mexicans. Racism and drug laws are inextricably linked. It has been argued that alcohol is legal today because it is the drug of Europeans—not because it is "safe" or "good." It is fair to say that drug laws have little to do with the pharmacology of the drugs themselves.

Today

Before prohibition of the opioids, there were certainly a lot of addicts, though by and large these addicts caused no social disruption and they lived reasonably happy and fulfilling lives. At the time, opioid addiction was considered a minor vice—much the way coffee or cigarettes are viewed today. Use of hypodermic syringes by addicts was almost unknown. The vast majority of opioids addicts drank their drug.

Today, when opioids are not only legally but socially vilified, the situation is far different. Most addicts do not ingest opium orally—they use heroin intravenously. This fact alone causes great problems, with the spread of disease and death from overdose and impurities. In addition, addicts must pay high prices for their drugs. For many addicts, this means turning to crime—a cost to society is estimated to be in the billions of dollars.

Chapter 3

Heroin Chic

Government officials have long been concerned about the glamorization of heroin. Recently, this took the form of an attack on the modeling industry by the president of the United States. More often, however, the concern is focused on the use of heroin by notable people in the various art worlds.

Pre-Heroin

Prior to heroin, notables who in a later time might have been junkies, used opium. Edgar Allan Poe and Thomas De Quincey are two of the most well-known opium addicts.

Even founding father Ben Franklin is known to have enjoyed the stuff. But life for them was very different than it is for the modern day user because opium was legal and considered to be only a minor vice.

Jazz

Probably more because of an accident of timing than anything, jazz, especially in the 1940s and 1950s, is associated with heroin, just as rock music is associated with marijuana. The number of jazz greats who were addicted to heroin at one time or another is seemingly endless. The ultimate example of the junkie jazzman is found in Charlie Parker.

Charlie Parker

The word "revolutionary" is inappropriately thrown around when talking about jazz performers, but in Parker's case the word exactly describes his impact on music. Quite simply, before Parker, the saxophone was played one way and after him it was played differently—and it hasn't changed much since then. Parker died at the age of 34. His death is usually attributed to the abuse his body took from all of the drugs he did, but it is more likely that he did a lot of drugs to self-medicate many physical ailments.

Billie Holiday

The story of Billie Holiday is tragic. While addicted to heroin, she drove New York club managers to distraction with her tendency to go home in-between sets, get high, and hang out until someone was sent to retrieve her for the next set.

The main problem that heroin caused her was not the drug at all but rather its illegal status. She was arrested on numerous occasions and, in 1947, spent eight months at a West Virginia work prison.

Billie Holiday died at the age of forty-four from heart and liver failure which was associated with her switch later in life from heroin to alcohol.

Switching to Alcohol

Medically speaking, there is no question that alcohol addiction is far more physically damaging than heroin addiction. However, because of the legal status of the two drugs, many heroin addicts—tired of being arrested and jailed—switch to alcohol with tragic results.

Not all junkie jazz musicians had such tragic lives as Parker and Holiday. Most, like less famous junkies, had a run of a few years and quit. Some, like John Coltrane, did so with relative ease. For others, quitting was more involved and ambiguous. Stan Getz, best known for his playing on *The Girl From Ipanema,* struggled with alcoholism for much of the rest of his life. Miles Davis was know to chip after his addiction.

Drawing by Carolyn Farris, from *Chaos & Cyber culture*

William S. Burroughs, the iconic heroin figure because of his lifestyle and pro-heroin writings.

The Beats

The Beat movement represented a kind of literary addition to the jazz scene of the 1950s.

Burroughs

The father of the Beats, William S. Burroughs, stands as

the iconic heroin figure. This is ironic given that he was as likely as not to be using codeine as heroin. His position of prominence in the junkie consciousness is due to three things: he wrote a great deal about being a junkie, including his novels, *Junkie* and *Naked Lunch,* he never disavowed the use of drugs even when clean, and he lived a lot longer than most people thought possible for a junkie. In its obituary of Burroughs, *The Village Voice* summed up his life, "Live fast, die old."

Lenny Bruce, known for "talking dirty" satire, preferred heroin as his drug of choice.

Lenny Bruce

Lenny Bruce marked a kind of conduit between the beat generation and the hippie generation. However, Bruce never saw himself in this way. He always identified with the old world of beat poetry and cool jazz just as he mistrusted the new world of rock music and collectivist politics.

When Bruce was arrested for obscenity over 100 leaders in the arts and other fields, including Theodore Reik, Norman Mailer, Richard Burton and James Baldwin rallied to his defense and signed a statement that described him as a social satirist "in the tradition of Swift, Rabelais and Twain."

Bruce abused many drugs throughout his life but his preference tended towards heroin. It is believed that he deliberately overdosed when he died in 1966.

Hollywood

Many people throughout the history of film have had varying levels of interest in the opiates. Errol Flynn was very engaged by the opium—although never to the point of becoming addicted. Recently Robert Downey, Jr. earned a reputation as being *the* junkie actor.

Bela Lugosi

Bela Lugosi is probably the most intense junkie in this group. Lugosi was addicted to morphine and methadone—the latter, because it could be acquired without a prescription at that time. The Lugosi-as-addict legend was heightened in the early 1990s with the release of the film Ed Wood. Although the film is not historically accurate, it does have one interesting element. Every time Lugosi injects morphine he becomes invigorated. This is a view of morphine rarely seen by the public—its energizing power for those addicted to it.

Movie poster from the 1935 film *The Dope T raffic*.

Junkies in the Moves

More than providing a who's who list of junkies in the industry, Hollywood has created many memorable fictional characters. Television glamorized junkies by making these ambiguous villains staple in cop shows of the 1970s. Since the 1990s junkies have increasingly decorated the dramatic scenery in Hollywood. Now it is quite common to use the "heroin overdose" as a convenient plot device to kill off minor characters.

Perhaps the greatest indication of heroin's importance in the modern movie is the number of characters who turn up that just happen to be junkies; sometimes they have minor roles as in *Suicide Kings,* and sometimes they have major roles as in *Pulp Fiction.* Junkies of all types still seem capable of carrying a whole film, though. A number of films about unrepentant junkies have surfaced as in *Drugstore Cowboy,* but the traditional Hollywood redemption melodrama persists as in *Permanent Midnight.*

When a movie needs a good "heavy" without the duality of a junkie, the non-addicted heroin *dealer*—scourge of both junkie and straight worlds—can be used to good effect as in *Lethal Weapon.*

Because of the mythic qualities that heroin has in our society and the resulting image of the junkie as both predator and prey, Hollywood will undoubetedly continue to use these images as fodder for its scenarios.

Today

Today, heroin continues to be popular amongst celebrities of the world. However, as always, it tends to be the negative side of heroin use that gets noticed. Although it was known that Kurt Cobain used heroin, it was his suicide that thrust this fact most distinctly into the public consciousness. John Belushi's speedball related death brought attention to his use. And Robert Downey, Jr.'s incarcerations have been widely publicized even though his actual usage patterns have never been made clear.

Chapter 4

Global Heroin Trade

One of the best known facts about heroin is that users pay very high prices for it. Given that it does not cost very much to produce, great profits are waiting for those who manufacture and distribute the drug. As a result, a number of criminal organizations are involved in turning poppies from farms throughout the world into heroin on the streets of the world's cities.

Global Distribution

In the old days, there was basically one route for world heroin.Opium from Turkey was delivered to France, where it was processed and then transported to the rest of the world—but principally to the United States. If this sounds familiar, it's because this is the plot of the movie, *The French Connection.*

This situation—a French heroin monopoly—caused prices to rise and purity levels to plummet. There was a long list of people who handled the drug as it went along the trafficking routes. This led, around 1970, to an average street purity level of 3%.

In the 1980s the heroin economy was joined by Mexican organizations, but these never made many inroads to the national heroin distribution system—except on the west coast of the United States where they established a near monopoly. In the 1990s the heavy hitters of the Colombian cocaine cartel entered the game.

Today, imports of heroin into the U.S. come from these three places, in the following order: Colombia, France, and Mexico. The end result of this competition is that at the dawn of the 21st century street heroin is very cheap and at its highest purity level ever.

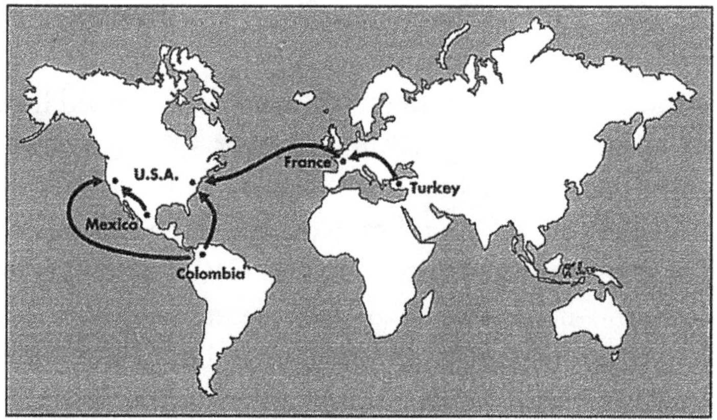

There are three worldwide distribution routes for heroin.

Heroin Manufacture

The manufacture of heroin, while not difficult for professional chemists, is not a trivial matter either. It involves three steps: Purifying the opium that is collected from the poppies, isolating the morphine, and converting the morphine into heroin.

Purifying Opium

The chemist starts by purifying the opium. This is done by first boiling the raw opium in water, causing the alkaloids to dissolve so that solids and other impurities may be strained from the mixture. The remaining solution is then heated over a low flame to evaporate the water. The paste that remains may be ingested directly or processed further.

The substance oozing from the openings of this cut poppy seed pod is opium.

Isolating Morphine

The chemist then dissolves the processed opium in boiling water and adds about one-fifth as much slaked lime as opium. Adding the lime converts the morphine into a salt—calcium corphenate—without having much effect on the other alkaloids. This is done because morphine—like most of the other alkaloids in opium—is not soluble in cold water.

After this new solution is cooled, the other alkaloids are precipitated out by filtering the solution through a coarse fabric like burlap to remove all of the solids, leaving just the morphine salt solution.

This solution is heated with about one-quarter as much ammonium chloride as the processed opium until the pH reaches 8 or 9. When this solution is cooled, the morphine will precipitate out. This solid morphine is filtered, pressed to remove excessive water, and then air dried. The result is a dark brown powder.

To further purify the morphine, it may be combined with dilute hydrochloric acid—making morphine hydrochloride—and activated charcoal and filtered repeatedly. This results in a white powder.

Converting Morphine to Heroin

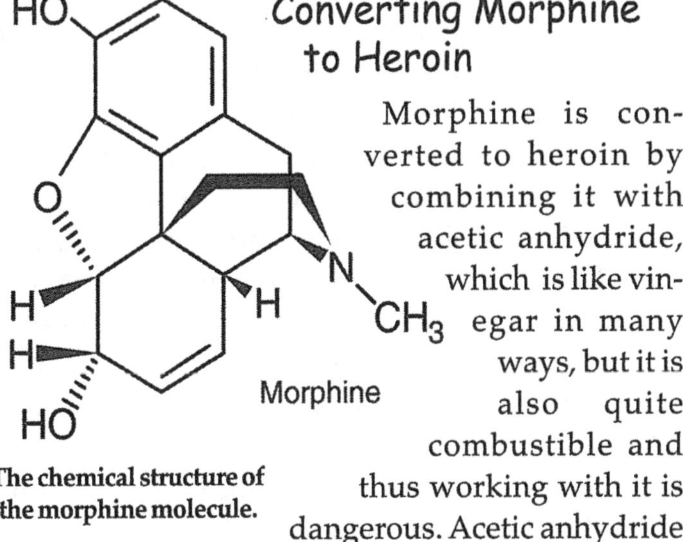

The chemical structure of the morphine molecule.

Morphine is converted to heroin by combining it with acetic anhydride, which is like vinegar in many ways, but it is also quite combustible and thus working with it is dangerous. Acetic anhydride is a controlled substance and is illegal to possess, because it is known to be used in converting morphine to heroin, but it is used for a number of other purposes and so can easily be acquired by clandestine chemists. The morphine hydrochloride is mixed with about three times as much acetic anhydride and cooked at 185°F in a gasketed pot to avoid evaporation. After roughly five hours, all of the morphine will have dissolved.

At this point, the solution is cooled and activated charcoal and about three times as much water as acetic anhydride are added. This solution is filtered until it is clear.

Twice as much soda ash as morphine is dissolved in hot water. This solution is slowly added to the morphine solution until it stops bubbling which causes heroin base to precipitate out of solution. The resulting solid is dried, resulting in a granular white powder. This procedure results in 70% as much heroin as the initial quantity of morphine.

The heroin base is finally converted to heroin hydrochloride—diacetylmorphine HCl. 2.2 L of ethyl alcohol and 110 ml of concentrated hydrochloric acid are used to dissolve each kilogram of heroin. Another 70 mL of HCl is added to the mixture. After this, the HCl is added very slowly—a drop at a time—until all of the heroin has been converted to a salt. This is the case when a drop of the solution turns Congo red paper blue.

When the heroin hydrochloride conversion is completed, another 4.4 liters of alcohol is added along with 3.3 liters of ether. The mixture is allowed to sit for 15 minutes.

Once crystals begin to form in the solution, 3.3 liters more of ether is added and the mixture is stirred and then covered. In about an hour, the mixture will have solidified. The process is completed when this solid is dried.

Chapter 5

The Science of Heroin

The study of the effects of opioids on the human body have provided profound insights into how the brain functions. In trying to understand why heroin and other opioids make users feel good, scientists have discovered important chemical processes which help regulate our emotions. Other discoveries have been made through the study of physical addiction.

Brain Chemistry

There are three important brain chemicals—neurotransmitters—that relate to heroin: dopamine, norepinephrin, and the endorphins.

Dopamine

Dopamine helps to control human appetites for both food and sex. Large amounts of this substance are also associated with being outgoing and exuberant. Parkinson's Disease and depression are related to having too little dopamine in the brain, whereas schizophrenia is related to having too much of it. Heroin, like most drugs that create a "high," causes a release of dopamine.

Norepinephrin

Norepinephrin governs the sympathetic nervous system—the nerves of the body that cannot be voluntarily controlled. Its primary purpose is to stabilize blood pressure above a minimum level.

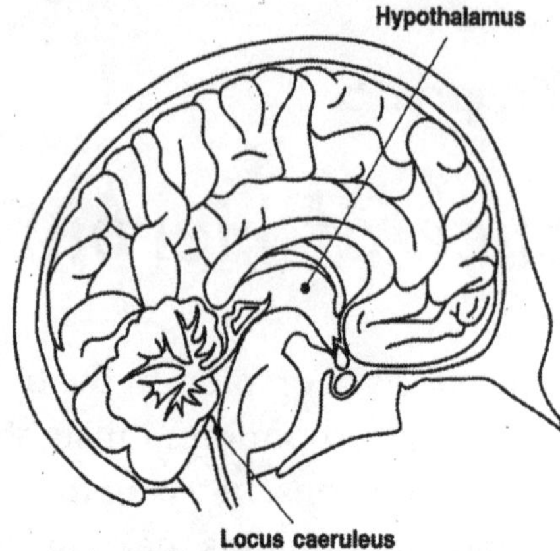

The human brain. Heroin acts primarily on the middle brain.

When a provocative situation arises, the brain's release of this substance stimulates the "fight or flight" response. Heroin depresses the middle brain—the locus coeruleus, in particular—and so provides the user with the opposite feelings: safety and contentment.

Opioid Receptors

There are sites in the body—primarily in the brain and spinal cord—called *opioid receptors* that are involved in happiness and feelings of safety. These sites were originally discovered by scientists searching for mechanisms that allowed morphine to cause pleasure and relieve pain. All of the opioids attach to these sites, where their effects are triggered.

There are at least five different kinds of opioid receptors, but only four of these are closely associated with the effects of the opioids: the *mu, kappa, delta,* and *sigma* receptors. The *mu* and *kappa* sites affect pain relief, the *delta* sites are involved with feelings of euphoria, and the *sigma* sites relieve depression.

Endorphines

It makes sense that the body would not have these receptors unless it created chemicals that would fit into these sites, and sure enough, scientists have discovered endorphins—morphine-like neurochemicals used by the body for many purposes, but primarily to modulate mood, promote pleasure, and manage reactions to stress.

The way that morphine differs from the natural endorphins—and there is some indication that the body creates its own morphine, not just morphine-like substances—is that it is possible to bombard the receptors with it, whereas under most circumstances the body only produces a small amount of endorphins at any time.

Physical Addiction

There is a certain puritanical idea that drugs are addictive as some kind of payback for pleasures they give. But this is not a scientific explanation. In fact, there is no reason that a drug must necessarily be physically addictive; some drugs, such as cocaine, are basically not.

Morphine is quite physically addictive, but it is conceivable that its chemical makeup could be changed so that it would only interact with the *delta*—euphoria—opioid receptor sites and with no other part of the body. It could be argued that heroin with out its addictive characteristic, would be a nearly perfect recreational drug. But as you would guess, there are no research funds available for this sort of study.

What Causes Addiction?

Surprising as it may seem at this time of modern scientific miracles, it is not known why the human body becomes physically addicted to morphine. There are literally dozens of mechanisms and explanations competing for acceptance.

Homeostatic Theory

The leading explanation is the Homeostatic Theory. In this theory, the body tries to maintain equilibrium, so those parts of the body that are depressed by the presence of morphine compensate for it after they become used to having it present. Thus, many parts of the body become hyperactive when the morphine is removed, providing withdrawal symptoms.

A good example is the constipating action of morphine. Once the body is used to the presence of the morphine, it attempts to overcome the constipation so that it may excrete waste as normal. When the morphine is taken away, this extra intestinal work results in diarrhea—a very common withdrawal symptom.

Tolerance

Tolerance to any drug effect is illustrated when the body needs a larger subsequent dose to achieve the same initial effect. How rapidly this takes place is a measure of tolerance, which may develop rapidly or slowly.

Tolerance is not a monolithic attribute of a drug. There are different tolerances to different effects of heroin, for example. The tolerance to its euphoric effects develops quite rapidly whereas the tolerance to respiratory depression develops much more slowly. The result is that people use more to get the increasingly allusive euphoria, risking an overdose because it takes a much lower does to depress respiration.

Bodily Effects

Heroin has a number of effects on the body. The most profound is the depression of respiration—the first effect of the drug that was noticed, even before its psychoactive nature was observed. This effect transfers to the fetus of a using woman.

Heroin was also noted early on in its history as an excellent cure for diarrhea. It does this by depressing the large and small intestines—there are many opioid receptors in the intestines. In addition, the secretion of stomach acid is decreased.

Heroin also constricts the muscles of the urethra and bladder which results in decreased urine flow, but also makes urinating itself much more difficult.

Long-Term Deleterious Effects

The long-term deleterious effects of heroin are few. For example, the liver metabolizes heroin but is little affected by it. While using, addicts may have problems with constipation, but that is about all.

Almost all of the bad physical effects of heroin derive from its legal status and, in particular, from the use of unsterile syringes.

Chapter 6

Heroin Subculture

People with a shared interest naturally seek each other's company. This situation is intensified when the shared interest is illegal. Heroin users, whose interest is both illegal and socially unacceptable even in most other drug circles, tend to form insular associations with one another.

Junkies

Just about everyone knows what the word "junkie" means: a heroin addict. The term is used loosely at times—sometimes to refer to any drug addict, but more often as a modifier to any habit-forming substance or act such as in the term "chocolate junkie." The term has a distinctly negative connotation in the straight world, but most younger heroin addicts use the term as a badge of honor.

Addicts who began in the mid-1980s and earlier tend to refer to themselves as "dope fiends," whereas younger addicts prefer the term "junkie." This probably derives from the common usage of the term in TV cop shows when the younger addicts were growing up.

Chippers

The term "chipper" is not well-known outside drug treatment circles. Just as "junkie" is derived from the heroin slang term "junk," so "chipper" is derived from the verb "chip," which means to use occasionally and non-addictively.

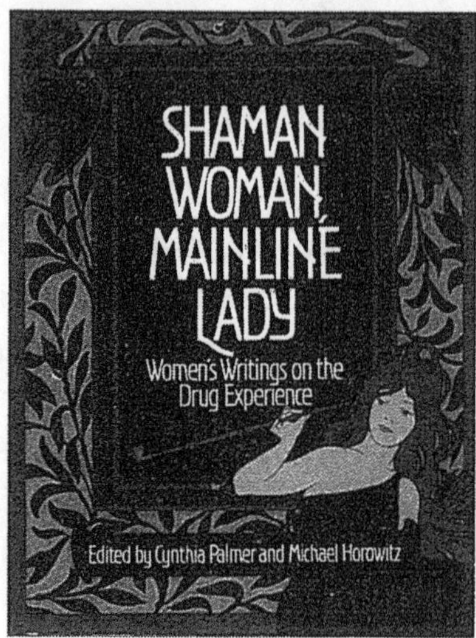

Historically , opium and its derivatives were associated more with women than with men.

There are many kinds of heroin chipper. There is the user of other drugs—especially stimulants—who uses heroin occasionally to come down, just as he may use barbiturates. Then there is the person who will use heroin if it falls into his lap but will not actively search for it.

Finally, there is the person who actively seeks out heroin, but who because of respect for the drug, or from fear or some other reason, does not allow himself to become addicted. This last kind of chipper is of particular interest, because there is very little that separates him from a junkie other than the procedures and rituals he uses to avoid addiction.

The very notion of an unaddicted heroin user was inconceiveable until quite recently. When a non-addicted user did occasionally pop up, he was dismissed as someone who was simply not addicted yet—that is, a pre-addict.

No quantitative research has been done on the percentage of heroin chippers who become addicts. It is known, however, that the number of heroin users in the United States is fairly constant over time and that there are roughly two million chippers and a half-million addicts at any given time. From this, it can be seen that the vast majority—80%—of users are not addicted.

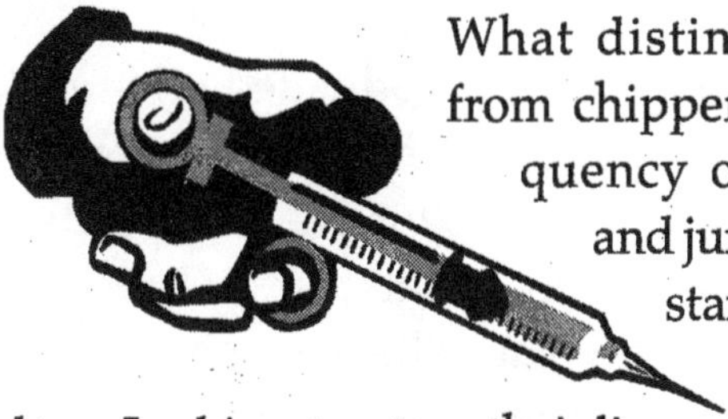

What distinguishes junkies from chippers is not just frequency of use. Chippers and junkies alike understand that heroin is a highly addictive drug. Junkies structure their lives around this doing what they must on a daily basis to feed their addiction. Chippers are similarly focused on the addictive properties of heroin and they develop or learn certain usage rituals which keep them safe from most of the drawbacks of the addict lifestyle.

Pushers

Heroin is a mythic drug and one of the great archetypes of its mythology is the "pusher"—an evil entrepreneur who forces drugs on weak individuals or tricks unsuspecting people into becoming addicts by giving drugs away initially.

Of course, this is not how people become involved with heroin—or with any other drug, for that matter. In almost all cases it is one friend who introduces another. This is usually done in the spirit of friendship, as in, "Hey, check out this cool new drug I've found."

Pecking Order

In the heroin subculture, there is a distinct pecking order which is determined by how far you are from the source of heroin. A good way to think of this is to visualize a number of concentric circles. In the center circle are the dealers.

Dealers

The dealer group can be subdivided. There is a distinction between a dealer who is buying ounces of heroin directly from Mexico for sale to street dealers and the street dealers themselves. Users care about this distinction, because they are going to get better deals from the "ounce" dealer.

Despite knowing this, however, most users do not actively work their way to higher level dealers. The main reason they don't is that doing so takes a lot of time and energy. A street-level dealer is not going to cut himself out of the distribution chain just so a user can get cheaper dope. The addict usually has more pressing concerns, and the chipper doesn't spend that much money on heroin anyway.

Junkies

In the circle outside the dealers are the junkies. These are people that have to spend a lot of time acquiring money. In addition, they may need to meet with a dealer a couple of times a day. As a result of this, they can't spend a bunch of time "waiting for the man." Junkies usually have many numbers they can call, and if all else fails they can score on the street—often at any time of the day or night. Sometimes a chipper will fall into this category, especially if he used to be an addict.

Serious Chippers

The next circle contains those chippers who are fairly serious about their drug use. They can usually score reasonably quickly but they don't have too many options.

Outside of this circle are the casual chippers who usually have no direct connections and must contact "someone who knows someone." The last circle—or perhaps it is a square—consists of all straight people.

Progression of Use

There is a commonly held belief about the progression of drug use, namely that people graduate from softer drugs to harder drugs. Details differ, but it normally goes something like this: alcohol, marijuana, cocaine, heroin.

It is not surprising that many people accept this idea, because it is precisely the order in which most people do take these drugs—with the possible exception of heroin, which most people never try. But this ordering has nothing whatsoever to do with one drug leading to another.

The order is the result of availability. How could it be otherwise? Marijuana use might lead to LSD use, since the latter is a more potent psychedelic. Similarly, opium use might lead to heroin use since the latter is a more potent opioid. But how is it that someone "graduates" from sedative hypnotic (alcohol) to a psychedelic (marijuana) to a stimulant (cocaine)?

Most drug users never try heroin, because they never knowingly have contact with the heroin subculture. Even very casual heroin users know of the extreme stigma attached to heroin, and by and large they do not want other people to know about their use. So when a person is introduced to heroin it will probably not be in the casual manner that one sees with marijuana—being passed a joint at a party. When a person is introduced it will most likely be by a close friend—or even more likely, a lover.

Chapter 7

Scoring

Sometimes a user may have a regular street dealer, but under most circumstances street deals are conducted between strangers. As a result, a user trying to score on the street has to simultaneously accomplish two very conflicting tasks. He must be noticed as a buyer to the dealers, but he must not be noticed as such by law enforcement.

Appearance

Drug dealers are a paranoid lot. They want to sell their wares to heroin users and not to police officers. As a result, anyone successfully scoring on the street tries to look like a junkie—even if he isn't one. So what does a junkie look like?

A lot of the stereotypes of the junkie are true. Junkies do tend to be thin—though certainly not all are. Junkies also tend to wear long sleeves but many—having found that most people don't notice track marks—don't hesitate to wear short sleeves. But perhaps the most important stereotype of junkies is incorrect. Junkies are not "out of it" and "half

A combination cigarette and syringe case popular amount rich ladies in the early 1900s.

asleep." In fact, they have a very active and fast-paced life. Junkies almost always walk at a breakneck speed down the street.

How the buyer appears on the street is a double-edged sword. He wants to attract the attention of sellers, but not that of the police. By and large, the primary concern of law enforcement is the arrest of drug dealers, but drug buyers are commonly arrested as a byproduct of dealer busts.

The only way that the buyer can limit threat from law enforcement is to spend as little time on the street as possible—both in terms of the amount of time on the street and the number of times he scores on the street. In order to assure a successful score, users try to get dealers' telephone pager numbers.

Pagers

Despite the widespread use of cellphones, even by drug dealers, pagers are still the primary means of communication between dealers and buyers. This is probably because pagers give dealers the upper hand in dealing with users, whereas cellphone numbers would allow users to call dealers anytime they chose. Pagers are used for drug deals in much the same way as they are used elsewhere. The buyer pages the dealer to some phone. The dealer calls back and the two agree on a meeting time and location.

In general, users get pager numbers from street dealers. If a dealer is particularly confident about a buyer (because he has often been seen or for some other reason), he will often offer a pager number. This just makes good sense for the seller. In order to buy on the *street,* both parties must meet up in a "hot" location—a place where drugs are known to be sold. With pagers, deals can be done in less volatile areas, often even at the buyer's house.

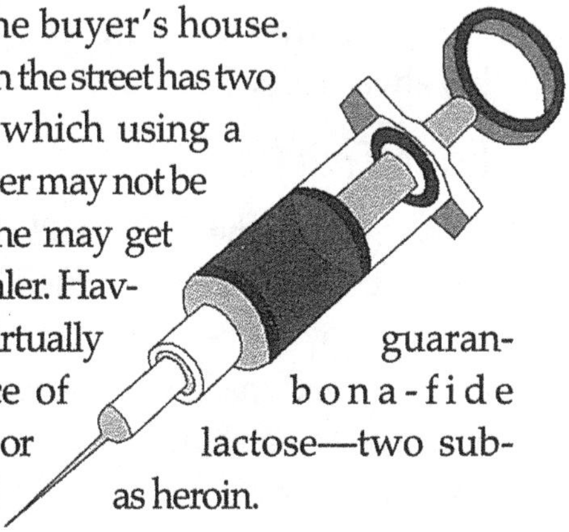

Purchasing drugs on the street has two main disadvantages, which using a pager eliminates: the user may not be able to score at all, or he may get ripped off by a fake dealer. Having a pager number virtually guarantees a constant source of bona-fide heroin and not molasses or lactose—two substances commonly sold as heroin.

Scoring Problems

Initially, having a pager number may present many problems to the user.

Call Back Phones

First, there is the issue of where to be called back. If the user does not have convenient access to a private phone, he will be forced to use a pay phone. Unfortunately, the vast majority of pay phones, especially in large cities, do not accept incoming calls. To make matters worse, a lot of these phones are not even marked as such, so a user may end up waiting around for call at a phone that cannot be called. With trial and error, "call back" phones are found.

Visibility

Another problem is a buyer may be made to wait a very long time on a street corner where it makes little sense to be waiting. This does not present a problem to the dealer, who will only stop briefly to pick up the buyer and then move on to another location, but it may cause locals to call the police on the "strange man who is hanging out" outside their house. Even if there is no problem with law enforcement, waiting is never pleasant; it may be hot or cold, but always boring.

Foot Traffic

Eventually, the dealers will come to the buyer's house. This is the safest situation for all concerned but, depending upon a number of factors, it may cause neighbors to take note and call law enforcement. The biggest problem is when strangers come to a particular house often and only stay for a short period of time.

Ethnocentrism plays into this, too. For example, a small group of Mexicans showing up in an all-white neighborhood is more likely to be noticed than it would be in a mixed neighborhood.

High Risk

The purchasing of heroin is the area of a user's life that is most likely to get him arrested. As stated above, under most circumstances police are mainly interested in catching dealers. Users are caught in order to find dealers or to provide evidence against dealers. But users still end up with felonies. Dealers will likely serve a lot more time in jail than users do, but as a narcotics career progresses, a user's criminal record will usually look as bad or worse than that of a dealer.

Chapter 8

Purifying Street Heroin

The impurities found in street heroin range from coffee to glass particles. Most impurities, like coffee, are harmless. Some users even enjoy these impurities. Coffee, for example, is tasted after injecting heroin that has been cut it.

Some impurities, like glass, can be deadly. To protect themselves smart users take care to remove the impurities from the heroin they buy. What follows is probably the most widely used method for purifying street heroin.

Particulate Matter

The use of cotton for filtration when heroin is cooked before being used is a small attempt at purifying the heroin ingested. But a much better job can be done with a little hydrochloric acid (HCl).

The user places about a gram of heroin in a small glass container—a test tube is preferred by knowledgeable users, but any glassware that will allow mixing will work. He then adds a couple of drops of 28% hydrochloric acid and allows it to react for a couple of minutes. Next, he adds 5 ml of distilled water and mixes vigorously so that everything that can dissolve does so.

At this point in the process, the heroin is in solution. The nonsoluble material in the container is garbage that the user does not wish to ingest. He lets the solution sit so that the particulate matter settles to the bottom and then pipettes out the solution, leaving the particulate matter behind.

The simplest kind of pipette is an eyedropper. If a pipette is not available, it is possible to pour the solution out of one container into another, being careful not to allow any of the particulate matter to be transferred.

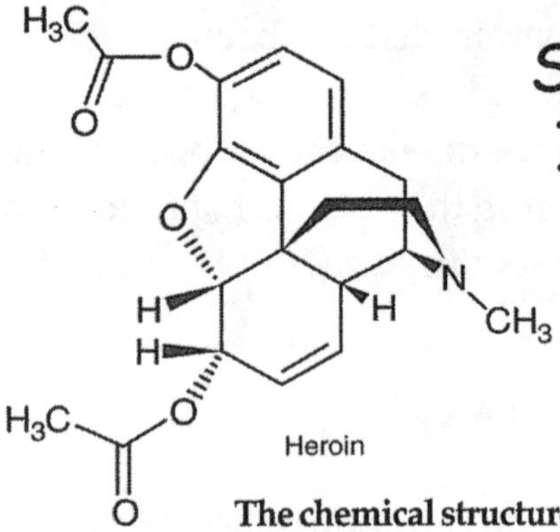

The chemical structure of the heroin molecule.

Soluble Impurities

The user next adds ammonium hydroxide to the solution, one drop at a time. This causes a white precipitate to form. The user continues adding the ammonium until he is certain that there is no more precipitate being formed. The solution is then gently mixed to assure that the ammonium is evenly distributed. At this point, the solution has a milky look.

The solution is then added to about 100 ml of ethyl ether—a chemical which experienced users handle with great care because it is quite combustible. This new solution is then vigorously mixed and left to sit. This will cause the water to settle at the bottom of the container. It is removed with a pipette and then discarded.

A mixture of 5 mL of HCl and 5 ml distilled water is created and added to the ethyl ether mixture. This is stirred vigorously for several minutes.

Afterwards, a water layer forms at the bottom of the container. The user then pipettes this out and into a small container such as a petri dish. The remaining ethyl ether solution may be stored and reused later on another sample.

Deacidification

The user then slowly adds baking soda to the solution in the petri dish. This causes the solution to bubble. When the bubbling stops, this process is finished. The resulting solution is then air-dried, which yields pure heroin and table salt (NaCl). The salt is harmless and may be ingested along with the heroin.

This process is also used by people who are interested in the purity level of the drugs they are buying. They simply divide the final mass by the starting mass.

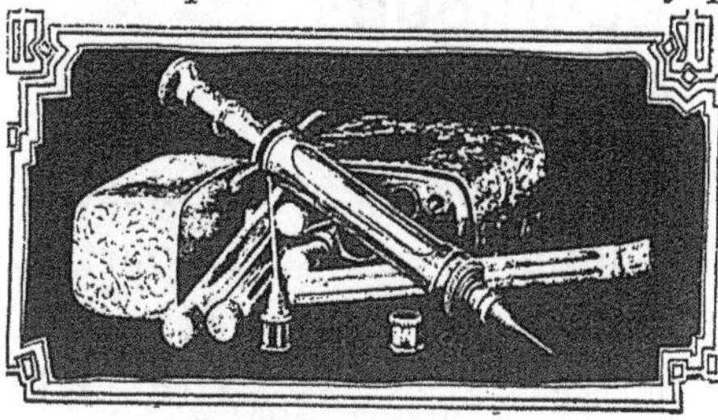

A syringe and related paraphernalia, circa 1900.

Chapter 9

How Heroin is Used

Probably the main reason for heroin's vilification is its association with the syringe. But it may be ingested in any number of ways. Heroin is probably more frequently ingested by inhalation (snorting) than by any other method. Another common method is smoking. Even when discussing injection, there are various methods. There are many factors that determine why a user chooses one method over another. This is true even for junkies; there is a commonly held belief that junkies always inject, and this is simply not true.

Different Techniques

There are three general methods of ingesting heroin: inhalation, smoking, and injection. There are other methods, of course. In particular, there is the anal suppository technique, made somewhat famous by the film *Trainspotting*. But these three methods are those commonly used.

Inhalation

Heroin comes in two forms: tar and powder. In powder form, heroin is snorted exactly as cocaine. The heroin is diced so that no large chunks exist in the batch. Then the drug is inhaled into the nose via some small tube such as a straw.

The procedure for inhaling tar heroin is much more involved. In this case, the heroin must be "cooked" as discussed below under Injection. Then this liquid mixture is sprayed up the nose with an eye dropper, syringe, or even a spray bottle if there is a sufficient quantity of the solution.

When heroin is distributed as a white powder, it is often snorted the same as cocaine.

Snorting

Snorting heroin is performed the same way that a user would snort any other drugs such as cocaine or methamphetamine.

Smoking

Smoking heroin, on the other hand, is not performed in the way that most people would think. Instead of burning the heroin directly, as is done with marijuana, it must be heated and thus vaporized. This vapor is then inhaled or smoked.

Probably because tar heroin looks like opium, it is smoked much more commonly than is its white-powder brother. But white-powder heroin may be smoked, too. In fact, both forms are smoked in exactly the same way.

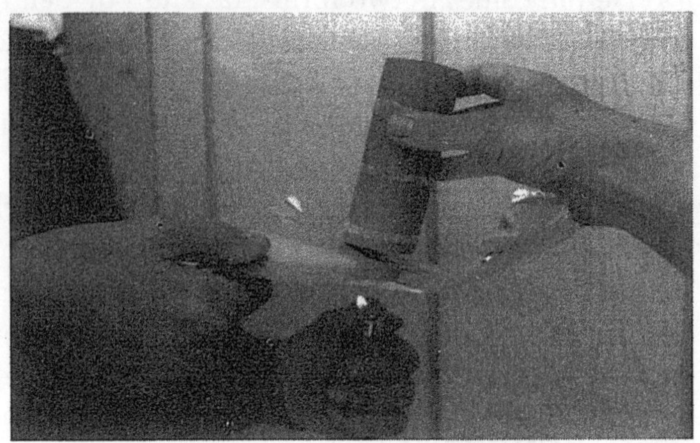

Preparing heroin to be smoked

A small amount of the drug is placed in the middle of a piece of aluminum foil. This foil is heated gently from below, in order to vaporize the heroin. The vapor is then inhaled, usually through some kind of tube.

In order to reduce waste, users generally use a large tube, such as a toilet-paper roll, but using such a tube requires two people because three hands are needed to hold the flame, the foil, and the tube. As a result of this, many users prefer to use straws, which can be held in the mouth.

Injection

There are three primary methods of injection. Heroin may be injected directly into a vein, referred to as "IVing." It may also be injected into a muscle, referred to as an "intramuscular injection." Finally, it may be injected subcutaneous, or just under the skin layer into the many small blood vessels that are present there. This method is commonly referred to as "skin popping."

Most new heroin users do not start out by injecting. Some do, however, because it is part of the thrill of trying "the hardest drug."

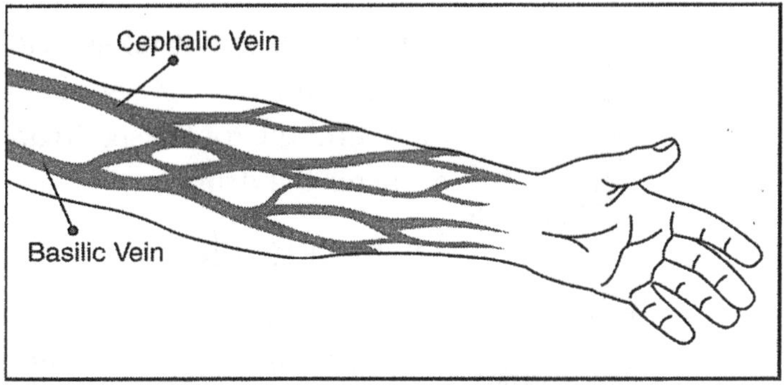

The main veins of the human arm.

Intravenous

There are various means of injecting heroin, but when most people think of injection they think of intravenous injection—injection directly into a vein. This method has many advantages to the user. First, there is no loss. This fact cannot be underestimated. IV injection is two to four times as effective as smoking. The second advantage is that it allows a very concentrated dose of morphine to be delivered to the brain. As a result of this, there can be a profound rush associated with an IV injection.

Dangers of IVing

IV injection also has a number of drawbacks. First, it is more associated with overdose and sudden death than any other method. IV injection also takes a good deal of skill to perform. Like all injection methods, it is very prone to the spread of disease if great care is not taken with the cleanliness of the environment and the tools used to administer the drug.

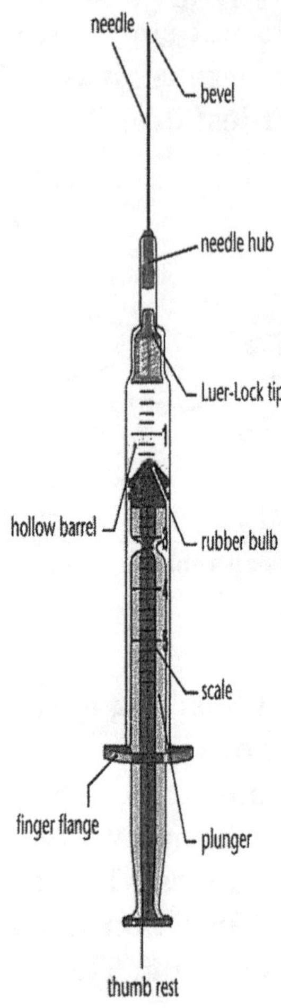

A hypodermic syringe.

Intramuscular

The intramuscular injection has the main advantage that it is easy to perform, but it also has many disadvantages. It is wasteful because much of the heroin breaks down into morphine and codeine before reaching the brain. It is also somewhat painful, as anyone who has had an intramuscular vaccination will attest. This kind of injection is also as prone to disease as any other method.

Subcutaneous injection is the middle road between the other two methods. It is relatively easy to do and less wasteful than injecting into a muscle. Below the skin layer is an array of tiny blood vessels, so the idea is to inject the heroin just under the skin layer.

Preparing the syringe

Before heroin can be injected—or snorted, in the case of tar, it must be dissolved into solution. This is done by placing the drug in a "cooker"which is just a subculture name for any kind of metal waterproof container. In a pinch, the bottom of an aluminum can may be used, but in most cases, the cooker is a regular household spoon.

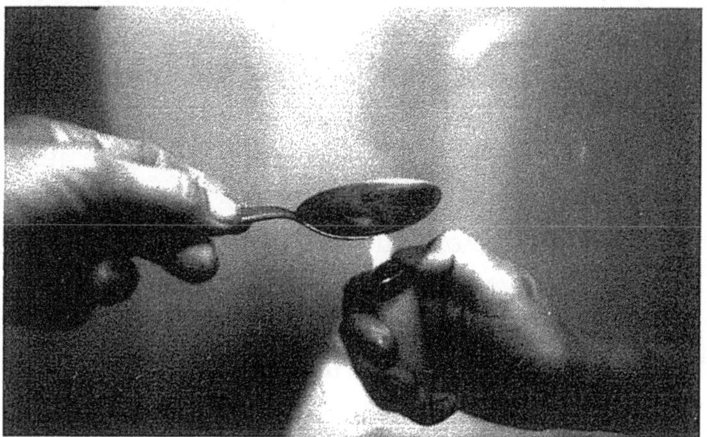

Dissolving heroin in a spoon in preparation for injecting it.

Water is added to heroin and the combination is heated to a boil and stirred in order to create a solution. In general, it is not necessary to achieve a boil, but this greatly decreases the risk of disease. This solution is drawn into a syringe through a small piece of cotton. The reason for this is to filter out any particulate matter in the solution, which may be harmful to the user.

After the solution is inside the syringe, the air is removed by pointing the syringe with the needle end upward and flushing the air, which will rise to the top of the syringe. There is a common misconception that air injected into a vein is deadly. This is true but it takes an enormous amount of air—perhaps a syringe full or more. But most users still try to minimize the amount of air that they inject, because there is no need to take a chance and it is part of the ritual anyway.

Subcutaneous Injection

For a subcutaneous injection, the user inserts the needle into a fleshy part of the body, most often the arm. A "pull back" is then performed. In this procedure, the plunger of the syringe is pulled out slightly. This creates a slight negative pressure, which will cause any blood that the syringe tip encounters to flood into the syringe. The syringe is then slowly removed from the body. When the tip is at the subcutaneous layer, the syringe will fill with blood. The user then slowly flushes the syringe contents.

Intravenous Injection

An intravenous injection is more involved, but is essentially the same as a subcutaneous injection. Users most often inject into the veins of their arms, but injecting into the hands, legs, feet, and even neck and genitalia are common. The first thing the user must do is to find a vein. It is very important that the user understand the difference between a vein and an artery. Most of the blood vessels on the surface of the skin are veins, but not all are, and injecting into an artery is very painful and dangerous. Since veins carry de-oxygenated blood back to the heart, they are blue in color. In addition, due to their lack of elasticity, veins do not pulse. This information is used by injectors when finding a vein.

The needle is inserted parallel to the vein with only a slight angle above the skin surface. When the tip of the needle is thought to be inside the vein, the user performs a pull back to ensure the location. Once inside the vein, the syringe contents are flushed.

Chapter 10

Disease

None of the major diseases associated with heroin use come from heroin itself. They come, instead, from its administration. Disease is more often associated with injection than with other methods, but the other methods do have disease risks as well.

AIDS

AIDS, which destroys the immune system, seems to be caused by HIV (Human Immunodeficiency Virus). AIDS doesn't kill anyone by itself, but it destroys the body's ability to fight disease. Most AIDS sufferers actually die from pneumonia.

HIV is a blood-borne pathogen transmitted via blood-to-blood contact. There are many ways that this can happen. Contrary to popular belief, it is possible—but very hard—to transmit HIV via kissing. This still requires blood-to-blood contact, however. Blood from one mouth must be transferred to the other and then interact with the blood there.

Being transferred via blood, HIV is readily transported when a user injects heroin with a syringe previously used by an infected person. It could also be transmitted via inhalation, but this is unlikely. Transmission via smoking is even more unlikely.

The use of clean ingestion equipment, especially when injecting, is critically important to safe heroin use. Most users know this. In states where syringes are legal, HIV infection rates for IV drug users hover around 35%. In states where syringes are illegal, the HIV infection rates can be over 80%.

Hepatitis

Hepatitis in all cases causes cirrhosis of the liver. A cirrhotic liver is dead. When its tissue is regenerated, it does not work as a liver. In particular, it no longer cleanses the body by removing toxins. Once completely cirrhotic, the liver does not perform this and other functions for the body, causing toxins to build up and eventually kill the individual.

Types of Hep

There are three principal kinds of hepatitis—denoted by the letters A, B, and C. Type A is the traditional hepatitis, generally acquired by eating food contaminated by animal—including human—feces. It is treatable with no irreversible damage. This is not the kind of hepatitis that heroin users worry about or contract as a result of their heroin use.

There are only two things that distinguish Type B hepatitis from Type C. Type C is more aggressive, and it is currently incurable. Otherwise, they are the same. Like AIDS, hepatits B and C are transmitted via blood, so they may be similarly transferred.

Endocarditis

There are two kinds of Endocarditis. The first is only a condition of concern to those with congenital heart problems. It progresses very slowly. The other Endocarditis is of concern to all injecting drug users, but once again it is transmitted by the use of unclean syringes. Unlike HIV and hepatitis, Endocarditis is more associated with shooting up in dirty environments, because of the large amount of bacteria needed.

Endocarditis is a bacterial growth that forms on the inner lining of the heart valves. These colonies grow large enough for parts to break off and flow through the bloodstream, causing a number of minor problems. These colonies do not, however, grow large enough to constrict blood flow through the heart valves. They are deadly, in that they eat away the heart valve itself. If untreated, a suf-

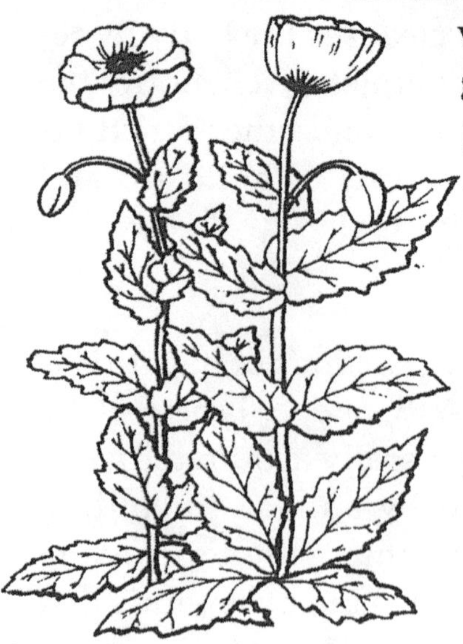

Blooming poppies.

ferer will die. Antibiotics will kill the bacteria, but in many cases, prosthetic surgery is necessary to rebuild the heart valve.

Other Diseases

Heroin users are susceptible to a number of other diseases of lesser severity. Snorters can literally burn a hole in the nasal septum. Heroin smokers can acquire lung disease, just as smokers of any substance can. Although this is a serious condition, heroin smokers rarely ingest a sufficient quantity of the drug to cause substantial problems. Injectors are prone to a myriad of minor problems, especially skin infections and blood clots.

Warning Signs

The diseases to which heroin users are prone are not nearly as important as the strong tendency—even amongst casual users—to avoid medical care. Chippers do not want to risk being labeled "addicts" and junkies know they will be. But it behooves all users to get medical care—especially when trouble occurs. There are many sympathetic doctors. In fact, the medical profession has a preponderance of morphine users.

The primary symptom, common to almost all major and minor diseases, is a long-term low-grade fever. Another common symptom that users should watch for is blood in the urine. Medical care is of great help, even with the incurable diseases.

Chapter 11

Addiction

Addiction is an important aspect of the lives of heroin addicts and chippers. Addicts must acquire a constant source of heroin or go through withdrawal. Chippers must use in a manner that will not lead to addiction.

What is Addiction?

There are three attributes that characterize an addictive substance: habituation, tolerance, and withdrawal. *Habituation* is a measure of how compelled a user is to ingest the substance. *Tolerance* is a measure of how quickly the body adapts to the effects of a drug. *Withdrawal* is the effect where the cessation of use causes the body to misbehave in various painful ways.

If any one of these three ingredients is absent, then a drug is not addictive. This definition—which is the standard definition from the World Health Organization—yields some surprising results. Cocaine, which is probably the most habituating drug known, is not addictive. Caffeine, on the other hand, is addictive.

Heroin is highly addictive. This is one of the reasons people have a great fear of this drug. It is impossible—or at least inappropriate—to say which of characteristic of addiction is the most significant, but in all three traits, heroin scores very high. It is quite habit-forming, especially to some. Tolerance develops very rapidly—even exponentially. Withdrawal symptoms can be quite painful, though they are almost never life-threatening.

Withdrawal

Fear and pain of withdrawal are the main reasons that junkies give for staying junkies. In the long run, it is seen—even by them—as a lifestyle choice. But withdrawal is an unpleasant experience even when properly medicated.

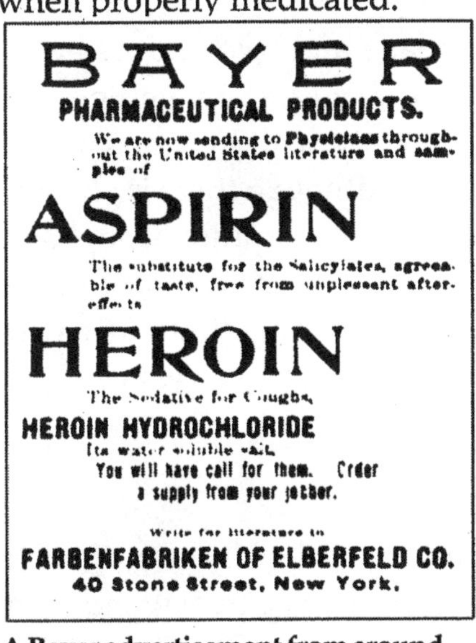

A Bayer advertisement from around the turn of the century . At that time aspirin and heroin were the two flagship products of Bayer .

The list of withdrawal symptoms is almost endless. Indeed, many symptoms claimed are almost certainly the result of withdrawing addicts' tendency to blame any discomfort experienced during this period on the withdrawal. In addition, since addicts have been on a constant dose of a powerful analgesic, the lack of the drug may cause a long-term ailment to finally be felt. But there are clear and severe withdrawal symptoms.

Insomnia

No matter how bad any other pain of withdrawal, the one thing that makes the entire process particularly hellish is the extreme insomnia experienced by the addict. Withdrawal has often been characterized as a bad case of the flu. This is partly true, but to this flu must be added the inability to sleep through the course of the disease, as well as a clinical level of depression. After three days without sleep, the withdrawing addict is exhausted and often frustrated to the point of tears.

Diarrhea and Vomiting

The most spectacular—and best-known—withdrawal symptoms are diarrhea and vomiting. Surprisingly, these are the only withdrawal symptom that are life-threatening. Although there is always a small chance of death from a ruptured esophagus whenever a person vomits, the main concern is dehydration. In the absence of any medications, a withdrawing addict should ingest as much water as possible.

Cramps

Muscle cramps and restless legs are often reported by addicts to be the worst part of withdrawal. This is partly because of the fact that while most symptoms are cyclical—coming and going over time—body aches are constant, often persisting, though to a lesser degree, long after the other symptoms have vanished. Restless legs are the phenomenon where the sufferer cannot release the tension in his legs. This effect is usually short-term—lasting only about 12 hours.

Depression

The least-mentioned aspect of withdrawal is probably also that which makes relapse so common: depression. Because the addict is so used to getting his endorphins exogenously (from the outside), the endogenous (inside) producing mechanisms of the body are disrupted.

It takes roughly five days without heroin for the body to start producing endorphins normally. It may take two to three weeks for endorphin levels to return to normal. During this time, the addict will likely be in a deep state of depression.

The most noticed withdrawal symptom is minor: a runny nose. This, along with watery eyes, is about the first symptom noticed. There are many other—real but minor—withdrawal symptoms, such as crawling skin. But these are not of much concern to the withdrawal sufferer given the other things that are happening to his body.

Avoiding Addiction

In order to avoid addiction, a chipper must know two things. First, he must know how often he can use. For example, can he use every day, every other day, or how often? Second, he must know how long he can use continuously. For example, can he use con-

Drug use is a frequent subject in mainstream films.

tinuously over two days and remain unaddicted? These are not questions that medical science has had much interest in addressing. Fortunately, users have been privately experimenting with their own bodies on this question for almost 100 years.

3-Day Limit

There are endless variations on the procedures that serious chippers use to avoid addiction, but they are all similar. For example, it is generally believed that three days is the longest continuous period that someone can use without bringing on quite noticeable withdrawal symptoms. This folk-wisdom agrees very well with hospital studies involving morphine. Even after only three days, almost all users experience profound insomnia, but there are many factors that will affect this and most users make a point of using no more than two consecutive days.

Drying Out

After use, the body needs time to adjust. Generally, this means that the chipper will refrain from using for twice as many days as he used. This fits in very well for the "weekend" chipper who uses only Friday and Saturday and then has five full days to "dry out."

There is some question about how frequently a chipper can use. It is often stated that a chipper who uses only every other day will not get addicted. But many who do so end up with a small habit. As a result, users are generally relegated to using at most once every three days. This, of course, goes along with the rule above about twice as many days off as on—one day on and two days off.

What these procedures and limitations show—and what long-time chippers know—is that it is not possible to use heroin very often and stay unaddicted. But for those who love the effects of this drug, it is the price that they pay. Non-addicted users almost certainly derive more pleasure from heroin than do addicts. Except for very brief periods of euphoria and contentment, addicts mostly receive pain relief from heroin. For the chipper, heroin is always new—or at least, mostly so.

Chapter 12

Detox

There are four primary means by which an addict may withdraw from heroin addiction: cold turkey, opioid substitution with methadone, Clondike, and antagonist therapy. Most of these treatments can be self-administered, but professional medical care is usually advised.

Cold Turkey

The standard detox method is cold turkey. That is, with nothing at all—just surviving the experience. Addicts inevitably experience this to some extent when they cannot locate drugs or when they lack money. As a result, they tend to want to avoid it when they decide to detox. But when there is no other option, it will work. The only thing the addict must remember is to ingest an adequate quantify of fluids.

The California Poppy . Although not a true poppy , morphine is nonetheless found in its seed pod.

Opioid Substitution

In terms of ease of detox, nothing beats opioid substitution. The most prominent substitute is methadone. There is a big distinction between substitution and maintenance. All over the country there are methadone maintenance clinics. The idea of these clinics is to substitute the heroin addiction with a methadone addiction. The theory is that by being provided a legal supply of the drug—or a similar drug—the addict will be allowed to live a normal law-abiding life, just as a diabetic might.

Why Methadone?

The question is naturally raised: Why not just give the addicts heroin instead of methadone? There are two primary reasons for this. First, methadone is long-acting, so it need be administered only once per day—as opposed to the four-times-a-day habit typical of heroin addicts. Second, methadone can be ingested orally with reasonable effectiveness, whereas heroin is particularly ineffective when ingested in this manner.

There are other reasons why methadone is the drug most accepted by the medical community. Since it is taken orally, there is no disease risk associated with it. And maintaining clients on high doses negates their ability to get high off of street opioids—in particular, heroin. But methadone is the choice primarily for administrative and organizational reasons.

The basic idea of opioid substitution is to use a non-morphine opioid to take care of the withdrawal symptoms so the body can detox from the morphine. But the substitute is not taken for long enough for the body to be addicted to it. If the body does become addicted to the new opioid, the patient is gradually weaned from it.

Mostly, addicts withdraw using methadone under a doctor's care. But some do it themselves. Methadone is widely available on the streets—mostly from people on a methadone maintenance program. The addict may also use another opioid that he has convenient access to, such as codeine.

Clonidine

The standard bearer for detox is often referred to as "Clonidine treatment," because of the importance of this drug in mitigating withdrawal symptoms. The idea behind this kind of therapy is that the withdrawal itself is not life-threatening—only painful. So a treatment that blocks the pain and symptoms should be as good as any.

This treatment modality involves taking a lot of pills. The most important is Clonidine, which depresses the locus coeruleus in a manner similar to heroin and so greatly reduces diarrhea, vomiting, and anxiety. It also lowers blood pressure and so helps the addict to sleep.

Clonidine alone will transform the nightmare of withdrawal into a bad dream. Just as important is its effectiveness at mitigating withdrawal symptoms, Clonidine may be purchased without a prescription in Mexico. Many people buy personal-use amounts via mail order from Mexican pharmacies.

Clonidine's ability to induce sleep is helpful, but much more is usually needed. This is why Clonidine is usually combined with some kind of sleeping pill—usually a benzodiazepine. The most commonly prescribed "benzo" for this purpose is Librium®. However, shorter-acting drugs such as Temazepam (Restoril®) and Alprazolam (Xanax®) are increasing in popularity.

In addition to these crucial drugs, a number of others are usually given for specific symptoms. In particular, Imodium® (a non-psychoactive opioid) is given for diarrhea and Tylenol® is given for muscle aches. This method is the ultimate in the "treating the symptom" philosophy of Western medicine—a philosophy perfect in some cases, such as heroin withdrawal.

The Iliad **—Helen of T roy of fers opium to T elmachus.**

Antagonist Therapy

The past few years have seen the popularization of treatments that involve the use of opioid antagonists. This kind of treatment is popularly called "rapid detox." However, there are actually two distinct treatments. The idea, basic to both treatments, is that an opioid antagonist is introduced into the body where it competes with the opioid agonists (morphine mostly) and dislodges them from the opioid receptor sites. This allows withdrawal to proceed much more quickly.

How it Works

In its purest form, the patient is anesthetized and the body is flooded with the antagonist. After four to six hours, the patient is completely detoxed—or so the theory goes. Condensing the entire—roughly five-day—detox period into a few hours means that the patient experiences almost unbearable pain and hence the need for medicated unconsciousness.

The main problem with this treatment is that it really doesn't work as promised—especially for clients with large heroin habits. After the treatment is over, patients normally suffer discomfort for several days.

Hybrid Treatment

A hybrid treatment approach combining antagonist therapy with Clonidine detox is becoming ever more popular in managed care facilities where costs—and time in treatment—must be minimized. In this treatment, patients are given larger than usual doses of Clonidine and the other drugs at the same time they are given increasing oral doses of the antagonist.

With this treatment, a patient can usually be released after three days feeling as good as he would after a week or more with the standard Clonidine regimen. The only real downside to this treatment is that some patients respond very poorly to it and suffer greatly despite the extra medication.

Chapter 13

Sudden Death

Without a doubt, the general public's greatest fear of heroin is its ability to kill the user suddenly in what is usually termed an "overdose." Although many people do die in this way, it is not as common as believed. Fewer than half a percent of heroin addicts die in this way each year.

Overdose

The list of famous people who have "overdosed" on heroin is very long. But the truth of the matter is that a true overdose of heroin is extremely rare. The problem is the tendency of people—medical examiners in particular—to claim a "heroin overdose" whenever a death occurs to someone who was under the influence of heroin.

An excellent example of this is found in the death of Janis Joplin. After a hard night of drinking, Joplin was very drunk. She ingests an amount of heroin which was apparently not very large, because she walked around the hotel for fifteen minutes afterwards. After this walk, she went back to her room and dies. The next day the newspapers proclaim that Janis Joplin died of a heroin overdose. Something is wrong with this picture.

Overdose

An overdose is a condition where too much of a drug is ingested. Scientific studies have shown that under normal circumstances it takes about a half gram of pure heroin to kill an unaddicted adult human by overdose. The result is asphyxiation caused by respiratory depression. In almost no cases do overdose victims ingest anything close to this amount of heroin although the high purity level of heroin today makes real overdoses much more common.

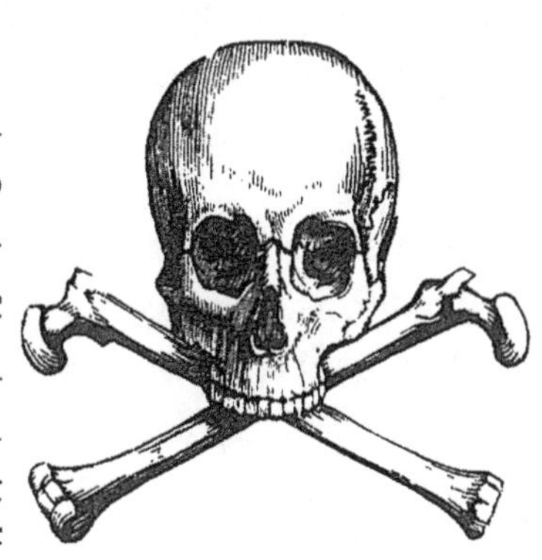

Heroin has long been associated with death in the public mind.

The one aspect of overdoses that is perplexing is the role of environment. What may be a regular dose at home may be an overdose in a strange place. As a result of this, users must be careful about where they ingest heroin.

Mixing Drugs

In a very large number of cases, death seems to be due to a mixture of different drugs. In particular, the mixture of heroin with central nervous system depressants is a lethal concoction.These drugs include barbiturates and the ever-present alcohol.

In the 1940s and 1950s it was well-known among addicts that they should not mix alcohol with their drug of choice. But around 1960, this important folk wisdom disappeared from the addict subculture and has only recently began to resurface.

Speedball

Perhaps the most reviled drug combination, the "speedball", is surprisingly benign. A speedball is most often a mixture of heroin and cocaine. Although it can be very dangerous, it appears to be no more so than cocaine itself.

Quinine

The sudden death associated with heroin very often occurs with pulmonary edema—the sudden filling of the lungs with fluid. This is also the case with an overdose of quinine—a common adulterant of white powder heroin. Speculation is that many deaths are caused by quinine overdose—especially in those cases where the heroin ingested is very small.

Another possibility is allergic reaction to the quinine or other adulterants. For this reason, many users purify the heroin bought on the street.

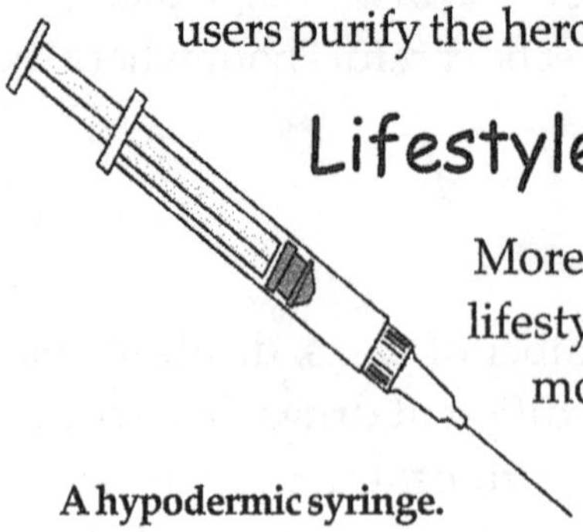

Lifestyle

A hypodermic syringe.

More than anything else, the lifestyle of the addict is the most dangerous aspect of the heroin experience. Addicts are forced to engage in dangerous activities to support their habits. In addition, they usually have poor diets and avoid medical care. In a three-year heroin maintenance program in Switzerland in the late 1990s, not a single heroin-related death occurred in over 1,000 patients.

Chapter 14

The Hardest Drug

Most experiences illicit drug users never try heroin because the very notion terrifies them. This is not such a bad thing, because involvement with this drug can wreak great havoc in the lives of people.

This extreme fear of heroin is part of what makes it such a dangerous drug. As we have seen, the drug heroin is in itself rather mild both in effects and dangers. When thinking about heroin we must not limit ourselves to the drug, but must expand our horizons to include *Heroin,* the mythical entity.

Danger of the Myth

It is the mythical status of heroin that causes the greatest harm. In the most simplistic terms, beginning addicts are usually pushed further into the heroin subculture even if they wish to retreat. In the heroin subculture they find acceptance, whereas in the rest of the world—even in other drug cultures—they are worse than pariahs. This means that those in trouble usually wait until their problem is much bigger—and widely known—before seeking help.

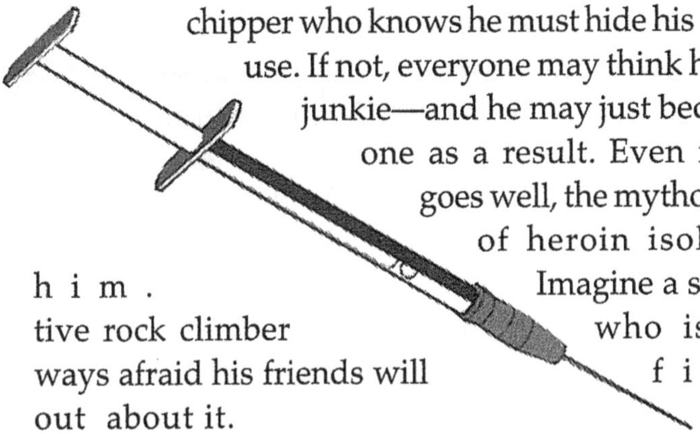

On the other end of this problem is the chipper who knows he must hide his drug use. If not, everyone may think him a junkie—and he may just become one as a result. Even if all goes well, the mythology of heroin isolates him. Imagine a secretive rock climber who is always afraid his friends will find out about it.

The very idea of one drug being "hard" and another being "soft" is unscientific and prone to hysteria and myth. The reason is that there is nothing objective that determines a drug's placement into one category or another—only vague notions based upon incomplete or incorrect information. What people mean when they say "heroin is the hardest drug," is that it is the most dangerous.

There are a lot of ways in which a drug may be dangerous. It may be dangerous because it makes the user a problem to others—he drives large cars too fast or gets into fights while intoxicated. Or it might kill the user, either suddenly, as with an overdose, or over time, as a result of irreversible tissue damage. A drug might also be dangerous just because it causes the user to make bad decisions about his life.

In each of these ways, heroin can be dangerous. But all drugs can be, and most more so than heroin. Heroin is almost certainly the most misunderstood drug. Like all drugs it has positive and negative aspects. Objectivity is important for users and non-users alike, because it can be the difference between life and death.

About the Author

Francis Moraes, Jr ., Ph.D., is trained as a research physicist and chemist. He was a physics professor at Portland State University in Portland, Oregon where he became interested in Portland's vibrant herion subculture—Portland is the number two heroin city according to DEA statistics. He spent several years studying this subculture in Portland, Seattle, San Francisco Bay Area, and New York City. Dr. Moraes has conducted substantial academic and pharmacological research.

Printed in the USA
CPSIA information can be obtained
at www.ICGtesting.com
JSHW020932191223
53963JS00006B/508